D0792142

Rock Music Library

Booking
a First Gig

By A. R. Schaefer

Consultant: James Henke
Vice President of Exhibitions and Curatorial Affairs
Rock and Roll Hall of Fame and Museum
Cleveland, Ohio

Capstone
press

Mankato, Minnesota

Capstone High-Interest Books are published by Capstone Press
151 Good Counsel Drive, P.O. Box 669, Mankato, Minnesota 56002
http://www.capstone-press.com

Library of Congress Cataloging-in-Publication Data
Schaefer, A. R. (Adam Richard), 1976–
    Booking a first gig / by A. R. Schaefer.
    p. cm.—(Rock music library)
    Includes bibliographical references (p. 31) and an index.
    Contents: A first gig success—Finding a first gig—Preparing for a gig—Performing a
first gig.
    ISBN 0-7368-2144-9 (hardcover)
    1. Rock music—Vocational guidance—Juvenile literature. [1. Rock music—
Vocational guidance. 2. Musicians. 3. Vocational guidance.] I. Title II. Series.
ML3795.S237 2004
781.66'023—dc21   2003004521

Summary: Describes the steps bands take to book a first gig, including making contacts,
finding locations for first gigs, and tips for making gigs successful.

Editorial Credits
Carrie Braulick, editor; Jason Knudson, series designer; Jo Miller, photo researcher;
    Karen Risch, product planning editor

Photo Credits
Capstone Press/Gary Sundermeyer, cover, 5, 6, 9, 13, 15, 16, 17, 19, 20, 23, 25,
    26, 27
Corbis/Steve Jennings, 21

**Capstone Press thanks the What's Up Lounge in Mankato, Minnesota, for their
help in preparing this book.**

1 2 3 4 5 6 08 07 06 05 04 03

Table of Contents

CHAPTER I

A First Gig Success

The band members appear from behind the stage. Bright lights shine in their eyes as they walk toward their instruments. The lead singer scans the crowd. He sees many familiar faces. He also sees about 50 strangers waiting for the band to start playing.

The band plays eight songs before taking a break. After the break, it plays eight more. By the time the band is done performing, the club is packed. The crowd cheers loudly for the band members as they walk off the stage.

Learn about:

Performing a gig

Making a gig successful

Finding a gig

Some beginning bands get gigs at local clubs or lounges.

Band members work together to make a first gig successful.

A few minutes later, the band steps out into the crowd. Friends congratulate the members. The club owner gives the band some money. The band members pack up their equipment and leave. They are happy with their first performance. They made some money, gained fans, and became better known.

Steps to Take

Many bands work hard before getting a first gig. Few beginning bands can book a gig on their first try. Beginning bands often need to make contacts, promote themselves, and work professionally to get gigs.

Many band members use their social connections to get a first gig. They talk to family members, friends, and people in the music industry. Once they have a gig, they practice and help promote the gig. The group shows up on time for the gig and plays a great show. Afterwards, the group gains fans and maybe even another gig.

CHAPTER 2

Finding a First Gig

Beginning bands often have difficulty getting asked to make a public performance. Band members who want a gig need to be determined. They should consider a variety of options for first gigs. A band's first performance might be at a school event, party, or a small club.

Making Contacts

Band members often get their first gig through someone they know. The band members talk to a variety of people. They may talk to owners of local clubs. Music store workers sometimes know of places that might work

Learn about:

Making contacts

Places for first gigs

Expectations

for a first gig. Established bands might be willing to help beginning bands find places to play. Music teachers can sometimes provide suggestions. Friends and family members can also be good sources of information.

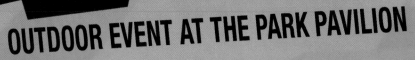

SPRINGFIELD'S
THIRD ANNUAL

SATURDAY
MARCH 21, 3 pm

BATTLE OF THE
BANDS!

OUTDOOR EVENT AT THE PARK PAVILION

Prizes awarded to
3 best bands!

Grand Prize = 30 hours
of FREE recording time!

SIGN UP AT CITY HALL
BEFORE MARCH 10

Cities often organize local "battle of the bands" competitions.

Locations

Many bands perform their first gigs in places other than clubs. School dances, mall openings, talent shows, and local festivals are all places that might work for first gigs. Some beginning bands play at a friend's party or a relative's open house. Some cities put on "battle of the bands" events. Several bands take part in these events. Each band is judged in comparison to the other bands. Winners may receive a prize.

Some clubs have amateur nights. Each performer who comes to these events has an opportunity to play. Amateur nights are a good way for beginning bands to experience what a performance is like. In addition, club owners can decide if they want to book a gig with a beginning band.

"Initially, popularity was a very startling experience. Coming out of small cafes and bars, acoustic solo gigs, and this scaled down, economical approach and then suddenly standing in front of thousands of people was very shocking."

—John McCrea, lead singer of Cake

Accepting Gigs

Beginning bands usually accept every gig they are offered. If a band gets a reputation for turning down jobs, it might not be offered very many.

As a band plays gigs, more people become familiar with the group. Well-known bands have a better chance of receiving more gigs. They usually can book gigs in clubs easier than beginning bands can.

" . . . people were coming out to see us. And they were paying my electricity and phone bills, so we decided to keep going. We just played wherever we could."

—Dave Matthews, lead singer/guitarist of The Dave Matthews Band

Bands work out gig details with
the club owner or event organizer.

CHAPTER 3

Preparing for a Gig

After a band receives a gig, the band members prepare for it. Bands that are prepared can relax and concentrate on putting on a great show. Band members decide which songs to play and then practice them. They also promote their gig and make sure their equipment is ready.

Promotion

Promotion is an important part of making a first gig successful. Bands who promote their gigs usually have more people come to them. Promotion

Learn about:

Preparation

Promoting a gig

Overcoming stage fright

Bands must practice before their gigs.

also helps people become familiar with a band's name. Many club owners appreciate the help a band provides with promotion.

Bands can promote a gig in various ways. Many bands post fliers on music store or school bulletin boards. Some bands put up posters at the site of the gig. Bands also may buy airtime on a local radio show to advertise a gig. Bands sometimes provide information about their upcoming gigs on the Internet. Some bands have promo packs. Promo packs usually have a tape or CD, a photo of the group, and information about the band

Bands can advertise their gigs on the Internet.

Band members can post fliers on bulletin boards to promote their gigs.

members. Band members can give club owners promo packs. Bands also may send promo packs to radio stations with a flier to promote an upcoming gig.

Equipment

Bands set up their instruments and equipment on the stage before a gig. They then check to make sure the equipment works properly.

Bands may take extra equipment to a gig. They can use the equipment if something breaks. Bands may take extension cords, guitar strings, guitar picks, drumsticks, and even backup instruments to a gig.

Professionalism

When bands perform gigs, they need to be professional. Band members need to arrive on time. They need to know their songs. A band that forgets words or misses notes probably will not be asked back again.

Bands also need to fill their playing time. If they are expected to fill 30 minutes of time, they need to have at least 40 minutes of music ready.

Sometimes, situations occur right before a band is scheduled to play. A guitarist may become sick an hour before the show. A club's spotlights may not work. Band members should always tell the event organizer about any concerns. The event organizer and the band may be able to work together to solve problems.

Bands members set up their equipment properly before gigs.

Overcoming Stage Fright

Some band members become nervous before a first gig. These performers can take steps to control their stage fright. Becoming too nervous can cause people to make more mistakes.

Band members can overcome stage fright in several ways. They can imagine being in front of a crowd while practicing. They also can imagine audience members enjoying the performance. Focusing on positive thoughts and breathing deeply also can help band members relax before a performance.

Checking that equipment is ready can help band members reduce stage fright.

Phish

The band Phish formed in the early 1980s. Members Trey Anastasio, Jon Fishman, and Mike Gordon met at the University of Vermont in Burlington. Page McConnell later joined the band.

The band's first gig was at a party. The next month, the group's members decided to call the band Phish. During the mid-1980s, Phish toured mainly in the northeastern United States. In the late 1980s, the group also toured the southern United States.

By 1990, the band had gained many fans. In 1991, Phish signed a record contract with Elektra. The band's CDs helped the group become even more popular. By 2000, Phish was known as one of the best jam bands in the world.

CHAPTER 4

Performing a First Gig

When performance time comes, bands need to make their gigs successful. The band members want to leave the event feeling that they have performed well and gained new fans. The event organizer should be happy with the band's performance. A successful gig increases the chances that a band will book another gig.

Good Impression

The reputation of a band depends on making a good impression. Event organizers and audience members who like the show will tell others about the band. More people

Learn about:

Making a good impression
Entertaining the audience
Payment

Band members must stay focused during gigs.

may come to other gigs. But if a band has a bad show, fewer people may come to other gigs.

To make a good impression, bands should show up on time and play what they agreed to play. They also need to be respectful of other people and equipment that they do not own.

Playing a Good Show

While performing, bands should try to make the show exciting. If band members look scared or bored, the crowd often is less enthusiastic. Some singers walk out into the crowd. Lead guitar players may dance on stage. Drummers may mouth words or make facial expressions. Some bands ask audience members to sing along to the music or to clap their hands.

Bands usually take short breaks at gigs. During a break, band members can talk to the audience or try to sell the band's T-shirts or CDs. They also may announce upcoming gigs.

Few gigs go perfectly. Band members need to expect that mistakes will happen and be prepared. One of the best things a band can do is handle situations professionally and with good humor. If a band member plays a wrong note, a joke can make the audience laugh and forget about the mistake.

A band can introduce its members to the audience during breaks.

Payment

Beginning bands usually get paid little for their first gigs. A small amount of money may be all the payment a band receives. But the experience of playing in front of an audience is worth it.

Band members become more experienced performers with each new gig.

As a band plays more gigs, it usually earns more money. Band members should promote themselves whenever they can. With each new gig comes a new opportunity to be a rock star.

Making a Flier

This list will help you make a flier to promote your first gig and draw more people to the audience.

 1 *Most fliers are on standard 8.5- by 11-inch (22- by 28-centimeter) paper, but they can be any size.*

 2 *Make sure the flier includes who is performing, where, and when. Include the address of the gig's location. You may want to include driving directions. Some people include a phone number people can call for more information.*

3 *Use a large type size that people can see from a distance. Do not use too many different type styles.*

 4 *Make sure all words are spelled correctly.*

 5 *The name of the band should be clear, large, and easy to read.*

 6 *A photo or a graphic attracts attention. Many fliers have a photo of the band.*

JUNE
21
7 PM
THE SMASH!
Performing at:
THE STARLIGHT CLUB
1254 N.LEOPOLD AVENUE
NEW YORK, NY 12405

Glossary

airtime (AIR-tyme)—the time that a radio station is on the air

flier (FLY-ur)—a printed piece of paper that tells about an upcoming event

gig (GIG)—a live performance in front of an audience

guitar pick (guh-TAR PIK)—a small piece of plastic or metal used to strum or pluck guitar strings

impression (im-PRESH-uhn)—what someone thinks of someone or something

promo pack (PROH-moh PAK)— a pack that usually has a band's tape or CD, a photo of the band, and information about the band members

promote (pruh-MOTE)—to make the public aware of a band's gig

reputation (rep-yuh-TAY-shuhn)—your worth or character, as judged by other people

stage fright (STAYJ FRITE)—the nervousness people feel before appearing in front of an audience

To Learn More

Belleville, Nyree. *Booking, Promoting and Marketing Your Music.* Ann Arbor, Mich.: MixBooks, 2000.

Black, Sharon. *The Gigs Handbook: A Beginner's Guide to Playing Music Jobs.* Evanston, Ill.: Benny Publishing, 2002.

Morgan, Sally, and Pauline Lalor. *Music.* Behind Media. Chicago: Heinemann Library, 2001.

Useful Addresses

Rock and Roll Hall of Fame and Museum
One Key Plaza
Cleveland, OH 44114

RockWalk
7425 Sunset Boulevard
Hollywood, CA 90046

Rolling Stone Magazine
1290 Avenue of the Americas
New York, NY 10104-0298

Internet Sites

Do you want to find out more about rock bands?
Let FactHound, our fact-finding hound dog, do the research for you.

Here's how:

1) Visit *http://www.facthound.com*
2) Type in the **Book ID** number: **0736821449**
3) Click on **FETCH IT**.

FactHound will fetch Internet sites picked by our editors just for you!

Index